Praise for *Gulf*

I read dozens of poetry books every year, and rarely have I experienced the kind of marrow-deep emotional attachment to new poems that I feel for Cody Smith's *Gulf*. These poems are filled with what the English poet David Jones calls "the actually known and loved," and by the end of the collection I came to know and love the ailing grandfather, an outlaw-Papaw singing Merle Haggard songs and teaching a boy to work on a tractor. I know and love the guns and the tools Smith's poems introduce, the mud of the ponds and the muck in the pirogues, and even the storms that threaten pretty much every day along the Gulf. The elegiac genius of Larry Levis presides over these poems, and other poets like Yusef Komunyakaa, Philip Levine, and Claudia Emerson offer some context, yet the whole is Cody Smith alone: singular experience, singular unforgettable voice.

—Jesse Graves

gulf

The Sabine Series in Literature

J. Bruce Fuller, Editor

poems

gulf

cody smith

texas review press | huntsville

Printed in the United States of America

Library of Congress Cataloging-in-Publication Data

Names: Smith, Cody, author.
Title: Gulf : poems / by Cody Smith.
Description: Huntsville, Texas : Texas Review Press, [2019] |
Identifiers: LCCN 2019011581 (print) | LCCN 2019014967 (ebook) | ISBN 9781680032031 (ebook) | ISBN 9781680031942 | ISBN 9781680031942 (pbk. : alk. paper)
Subjects: LCSH: Louisiana—Poetry. | LCGFT: Elegies.
Classification: LCC PS3619.M5733 (ebook) | LCC PS 3619.M5733 A6 2019 (print) | DDC 811/.6—dc23
LC record available at https://lccn.loc.gov/2019011581

Cover photo: courtesy fullcirclepiece on flickr.com

for Nichole,
who started it all

CONTENTS

CONTENTS

Ode for Delta Summers

So much of those summers scraped against cypress groves as we paddled the pirogue and prayed against storms. The mud-bogged Catahoula Lake bank would swallow James Larry's pickup like an egg in a snake's throat. Days ended the same: heat lightning, catfish pliers and fillet knife in my hand, my father in his workshop fumbling the knobs of an acetylene tank, him trying to talk to me through the blue-pointed whirl of a blowtorch, hunkering down to his work, hood pulled over his face, his flame gutting metal, labor and whatever wisdom I didn't hear sifted through the choke-cherry, lifted crows from their perch in the red oak, folded wasps and dirt daubers back into their nests while Mama and Grandpa cooked yesterday's catch in the fry shed out back, the sizzle of cornmeal hitting grease, wet air battered by fish musk, fried okra, the wild jasmine vine that ran the front porch posts. Lit citronella candles called the dusk home.

I

If I should leave you
Try to remember the good times
Warm days filled with sunshine
And just a little bit of rain

—FRED NEIL

Louisiana Wetland Elegy Taken Out to Sea

There's a hundred miles of bad road between here
and the Gulf of Mexico, but we don't say it.
We listen to Tab Benoit sing "When a Cajun Man
Gets the Blues," count the braille of cypress knees
sprouting from the gloom of swamp water as we drive
the Basin Bridge. When we cross over, we lose
the horizon, pine thicket crowding I-10,
and I think if I let my hand out the window,
I could graze the reflective orange vests
of the state workers bush-hogging the grass
in the ditches spiced with Miller and Bud cans.
They say now the maps are wrong, that the state
is no longer a boot, that the toes are cut off,
that the sole jags. There's a hundred miles of bad road
from here to the brackish slurry where the land begins
its dive toward the deep-water drilling wells,
but there used to be more. Tab sings about dancing
the fais do-do till he can't dance no more.
We'll soon be home, tucked away in fields
of sugar and soybeans. What's left of the boot
loses another football field of land
by the time we make it to Baton Rouge
from Lafayette. We unload our things. We sip
coffee under the porch lights, in this state
where flames from the refinery flare stacks
of Cancer Alley rise above the cane
and make lamps of clouds that overcast
the sky so often on fire and whose ground
kneels further down into water.

Elegy for a Trailer Hauled Off and Rotting Somewhere in the Deep South

—for Calee, nearly too young then to remember

Here, people burn gas for something to do, like how
    I drive Belah Road past the trailer my parents brought me

home to, how I wave at someone else's kids in that yard,
    a dog chasing them, nipping at their saggy diapers,

some different dog scratching fleas under the porch.
    The first trailer I remember living in was after my sister was born,

how we shared a room, how my mom and dad
    had to walk sideways to fit between my bed and Calee's crib,

how I would slip my hand through those veneered slats
    to hold her hand as she slept, would wrestle her over

into bed with me when she cried, the crayons smeared
    on the walls, hot sauce stains on the stove door.

Then the upgrade to the full-sized single-wide.
    The screened-in back porch where we'd watch

the early starlight of fireflies dogging bats at dusk,
    my dad's busted leather steel toe Redwings shaking

the four-a.m. stillness as he walked down the hall
    to kiss us goodbye and leave for work,

the tin skirting I helped him screw down that hid
    our house's wheels, the petunias and elephant ears

I help trowel in front of the tin. Or the one Nic lived in
before we married, that trailer park in West Monroe

past the houses off Arkansas Road with white columns
and wraparound porches, the bacon and egg sandwiches

she'd make us after waiting tables at The Coffee Bean
and I had showered off the blood and mortar dust

and sweat from laying bricks all day for new construction
up on Snob Hill, how she and her mom and Vonnie

and I would form a line down the hall waiting for our chance
at the one bathroom, the cloud of hairspray I'd always walk into,

their neighbor, Harry, drunk on his half-empty bottom-shelf fifth
of Old Crow and shirtless and singing Johnny Paycheck

to himself on his porch when I'd drop Nic off, his neck stretched out
as he stared at me kissing her goodnight. Even in elementary school,

I knew I should've been ashamed of it all, on display, then, with my hand raised
when asked *Who needs a free or reduced lunch form?* like Mom told me to

while she was putting her makeup on at the red lights on the way to school.
How after my mom and dad rotted the knot of their union and the movers

came to haul away my parents' last trailer, all that was left were some fleas,
a few cinderblocks, lost toys, and a set of front steps leading up
to nothing.

Heat Lightning

It rains every afternoon, and lightning clogs in the bowels
of storms that roll in like fireflies my son chases into the rising
cricket song. We wait in line at Hurricane Drive-Thru Daiquiri
hoping to beat the rain home. Later, when rain stops, the land
is reclaimed. In the minutes before the road sings its humid song
of steam, we drive golf carts through the subdivision sipping
our drinks, our pants rolled, shoes shucked. We eat our supper
on the back porch, loblolly spiking the day's falling light
as we spray our son off with the water hose. We believe
in this lightning. We watch it crawl over Cancer Alley and up
the Florida parishes, as it finally leaves us sitting into the night
with only the Dow Chemical flares stacks lit like candlelight.

Hurricane Parties

The weathercaster says board the windows. Gusts somersault
    brackish water and tupelo like postcards signed in wet cursive.

LaSalle is a dry parish, so we drive to the Caldwell line
    for Jim Beam, Old Crow, Boone's Farm. We sit on ice chests

of beer, take turns flipping meat on the pit. Birds fly
    without flapping their wings. Someone puts Dr. John

on the radio. Wiping smoked sausage grease from our mouths,
    we sing "Gris Gris Gumbo Ya Ya." Spanish moss wind-flung

from oaks carries this drunken séance down the road. The wind
    turns the table umbrella inside-out, whistles through the lattice

of porch furniture. The power dies. Candles and lanterns wander
    houses, flames turning faces sepia. Soon we'll stumble into the yard.

Lifting our drinks, we'll toast what's to come and what's to pass.
    We'll lean forward, raise ourselves by our toes to sea-level.

If tornadoes sound like train whistles, this is more like old shoes
    banging in the dryer, your parents falling asleep to AM static.

When the eye arrives, we'll walk the road to check on the old folks,
    fetch limbs, road signs, and mailboxes from the ditches.

Soon we'll gnaw the flesh inside our mouths.
    Soon we'll put our hands to the wall again.

Flash Flood, Mid-August Baton Rouge

Our little girl who still needs a name swells my wife's stomach
as she lobs side to side in the bed. They say this is sleeping weather:
rain and thunder from named hurricanes leaving the Gulf of Mexico.

We flip our phones facedown and sleep under a light-drunk sky.
The pond bloats to birth water that'll crawl through our home.
Our little girl who still needs a name sleeps during the day and kicks

through the night. We take our coffee on the back porch and sit close
to the wall away from the rain. The whole atmosphere swirls under
a tropical depression the Gulf of Mexico brought to life.

Gusts lean the pond fountain side-to-side like a Cajun two-step.
Last night was the Perseids' peak. Today the storm is on every channel.
Our little girl who still needs a name swells my wife's stomach,

nearly pulls open ribs groping for softer flesh while the pond climbs
its banks and morning births a sunrise over a pulled string of pine tops
that bend under this storm the Gulf of Mexico brought to life.

We'll leave this flood in a few weeks, put 2,000 miles
of country between us and these Acadian parishes,
my wife with our little girl in her stomach who still needs
a name and storms in the Gulf needing the same.

Eating Fried Chicken at Uncle Albert's Restaurant

Mid-morning, and your father and Spanky already sweated
through their shirts, dust-clung forearms wet with work,
the whirl of the shop fan through its busted expanding metal face.

Your father built rockers and swings, so many front porches
marked by his craft, and even now your fingers remember
the feel of the tape measure you held for him, and you still see him

reach for the pencil pinned behind his right ear and whittled
down to a point by a bone-handle pocket knife.
You knew work, but rarely understood how to get it done,

so much math and geometry wrestled for years. Some days
he'd let you shoot the nail gun, the kuh-chunk
of its blast hollering wind across your face. At noontime,

you and him and Spanky would knock off and order
fried chicken at Uncle Albert's Restaurant and eat
with the town's mechanics and Justice Oil field hands.

Every man's name printed on their shirt. Every man beautiful
in life's routine, in what's left after toil, beautiful knowing
they'll go home to acreages of land, mobile homes butted against

hardwood or set behind pine skirted by raked mounds of their own needles.
A person works all their life to put their name onto something:
sometimes a mailbox, a business card, a bible, sometimes a shirt.

Gulf State Elegy Unfolding Under Evacuation

On HWY 155, the pickup engine croons
almost on pitch with Clifton Chenier
& His Red-Hot Louisiana Band.

Your children are asleep in the back,
your wife on her phone in the front.
A pizza box wedged
between the windshield and dash,
red sauce smeared over your boy's skulked jowls.

Driving through this town's speed trap,
you can roll
down the windows,
listen to the chaff of a bad harvest scorch.

Months from now, your kids will sleep like this again
on I-10 heading to Tallahassee
from Baton Rouge after a hurricane—

You can roll your windows down there, too, hear
the tree frogs and crickets whine about the steamed air.

But today,
hurricane season is still cutting its teeth
off the coast of Africa,
some accordion tune squeezes through the speakers,

men in white rubber shrimping boots drag nets
through flooded ditches for crawfish,

two boys in a pirogue run trotlines for catfish,
            wallop with a child's baseball bat
alligator gar hung on the line.

                                                The lady at the counter
will upsell you the bigger soda, will sing along
to Christian radio while ringing up your beer and gas.

This sorghum by the road smells like the sweet feed
your Appaloosa ate all summer,

the grain field nearly close enough to scratch
            your syrup-colored fingers that rudders this wind.

                        You'll come back here an evacuee
            from storms you've always known,

will fill gas cans and propane bottles at some Cajun gas station
            that sells crickets outside by the ice bin
and nightcrawlers inside by the Natural Lights and Old Milwaukees,
            will strap what you have down in the bed of the truck
                        and leave this place you've always left.

Farmers will harvest those acres of sugar cane after you leave,
will disc and till what the machines miss.

After the storm, interstate traffic will stop for hours.
You'll crack the window and the dusk-moan
            from across the ditch will pull your eyes back.

Your son will stir in his booster seat with the growing pains
of broiling blood that melts the welds of bone
in his legs, your wife unbuckled
stretching a bottle of formula in the direction
of your daughter's wails.

But today, you are not leaving.

The combine blades haven't hounded the jackrabbits
and field mice through the cane.

The Mississippi River, the Amite, the Tangipahoa,
the Chattahoochee will all rise and fall, but now

as you cross The Basin Bridge, a tugboat putts
beneath you down the Atchafalaya
as your son wakes and asks, *Are we almost home?*

and you look back at him and still know where that is,
will still have the right thing to say, the horn blowing
behind you rising from muddy water running
toward fantail tributaries and salted oil slicks in the Gulf.

Elegy for the Pond

which yellow jackets, a red Hereford bull,
        and the neighbor's rabid mutt ran

us into, where we brought cane poles for bream
        fishing and shotguns for water moccasins.

The one the ice only took once, and the pond
        Dusty shuffled across and toppled under,

and from the bottom, he looked up through
        the opaque cloud of ice, copper and crimson

stains haloing dead leaves trapped in the broken
        sheet, rays of light falling through,

like some church's leaded glass coloring
        what's on the other side. The one

from which he crawled back out, his body
        a Pentecostal tongue. The one where

we baptized our six-year old selves, afraid
        of what sin might be, waded year after year

a bit farther to dunk each other into the red water,
        minnows eating flakes of sunburned skin

from our backs. How short, those days the breeze
        dried our muddy hair under June skies stitched

with jet contrails while the king snakes sunned on Hanger Road
        under those bats that were charred coals orbiting the sunset.

A Stranger Remembers Watching *Lonesome Dove*

The world spirals far-flung and loose
past his eyes, those two bruised baby tomatoes

dripping down his cheeks. He snaps the buckles
of his Old Liberty overalls by feel, tests the buttons

of his shirt against receding fingerprints—
not much else has stayed with him these seventy years.

We'd watch *Lonesome Dove* on the box TV that sat
on the living room floor of my childhood. By the time

Woodrow had cursed Gus's damned vanity, he'd be in tears,
wiping his eyes with a bandana sweat-soiled and holy

and Robert Duvall's chest dropping then flat. There's a picture
in a Christmas popcorn tin of us on his front porch,

him fingering a D chord on an acoustic guitar, mouth broke open,
drooling tobacco spit and the words, surely, to a Haggard song,

me beside him, head just jutting out from behind his spare
guitar, arms blurred by the strum, summer-scraped knees,

those bare toes with hardly any miles on them. I can paint you
my leaving: crows cawing above him as he feels

for the porch's railing, then the piece of him visible
in the few inches between car roof and luggage.

I could brush in my own hands that pulled the gear shift
        into second, the other hand honking the horn as he waves,

but I only hear, *I've got to get down the road and pick up a few last boxes.*
        The longer I wait, the longer the drive, and see him shifting his body

toward the sound of my voice, eyes uselessly opened.
        Don't be a stranger, you hear? He asked. *No sir, I don't suspect*

I will be, I called from a car pulling onto a road
        leading west that stretches like marks in skin.

Elegy Uprooted from the Wet Soil

—for Connie West

Where you are, the birds won't shut up about morning,
        and there's dew on the swing and steam gurgling

in the coffee maker. Somewhere else, I'm asleep,
        tin foil over the windows, a box fan grinding

on the floor. Let's call it six hours. Let's call it Tallahassee
        from Baton Rouge. There's not enough rivers to cross

and the ocean's out of reach from I-10. The alarm
        clock clicks before the ring. Let's say the kids slept

through the night in their own beds, say legs stray
        from the covers. There's too many dirty diapers

in the living room. There's too many dishes in the sink. Say
        the birds are jazz, and I won't explain it. I'm writing you

a letter while the turntable spins John Prine singing about flies
        buzzing in a kitchen. They light in the sink, scratch their legs

over last night's rice and beans. The sun sets sooner here,
        reminds me there's a second chance to call. Let's say

these tree frogs above my dusk-wet grass and those bats
        in the sugar cane past your front porch light sing the same

song across these phone lines. Let's wait to say that we've got
        to go, wait to say the mosquitoes are carrying us away.

2

Undertaker, please drive slow.

—WILL THE CIRCLE BE UNBROKEN

Up and Over the Mountain

—after Richard Hugo

Well, Dick, you're right. The car that brought me here
still runs but it ain't happy about it—

the clutch nearly gone, the cry of that fan belt
like a whooped child. Dick, I'm afraid to roll

down the windows since the fast-food incident:
steering with my right knee, clutching with my

left foot, shifting with my right hand, manhandling
the stuck window up with the left. My Lord,

my son might freeze in the drifts. I give him
my fear of heights. He gives it back and takes

mountains. Dick, once you're over some hills,
you're done. I don't think the car will again

climb that divide. Where does it all go, Dick? All this
leaving. All this returning upstream to something

no longer yours. Sometimes I don't answer my grandmother's
calls for days, afraid it's to tell me to buy a belt

and black shirt and plane ticket. Dick, you know
we vulture the passing. Who gets the tractor,

the tiller, the pearl-buttoned Wrangler shirts,
the Bible, the Old Timer

pocket knives, those few acres that are all
        you know till you're older? I've already taken

a pair of his old glasses. They look just like mine,
        and I put them on some mornings when the grog

still lumbers my veins. It takes a bit, usually
        the first pot of coffee, to realize I can't see,

that the prescription is off, that the lenses
        are speckled with red garden dirt.

Picking Up Cans

When granddaddy's hands still worked,
they shelled bushels of peas.

I'd ask him, *Why not drive them*
up to W.G.'s place and run
them through a machine?

There's no rhythm in it, son.

People sing Lead Belly in the Delta. Twelve bars
shuffling a palm mute chug that bogs down
into the black LaSalle Parish mud.

Insects flocked his cup of tobacco spit
those days on the front porch,
abuzz and pouring down like Sunday revival,

his feet tapping behind the beat as he hummed
Haggard's "Workin' Man Blues."

He would crawl the ditches
out on Hanger Road and Tom John Drive
for soda and beer cans tossed from vehicles,

his truck bed stacked with garbage sacks stuffed
with crushed aluminum, and we were on our way
to the recycling center for our big payday.

A pouch of Levi Garrett tobacco in his shirt pocket,
the pocket calendar stuck to the Ford's dashboard,
the day ripped off and held out the window
cracking the burnt air like a metronome out of time.

Elegy for the Family Tractor

In 1950, my great-granddaddy broke her in
then passed it on to my grandfather who gave it hell
these last fifty years yelling, *You bastard. I don't give a good Goddamn*

if you ever turn over again. All those days
he seasoned the earth with salt dripping from his chest
crooked over the tractor's gnarled machinery: the corroded

spark plugs, flooded carburetor. Rusted out linkage and cams
oiled down or else walloped with a wood-handle ball-peen hammer.
The days he's in his right mind, he'll ask about the jalopy

that's now put out to pasture with my sorrel mare.
The days when fog crawls the decades in his mind, he yodels
from his bed the work songs I mimicked, the summers

my stretching bones burned my body walking the turnrows,
him standing under a straw hat varnished in dust and sweat,
a decade older then than I am now and moving away from me

down the lines like Jimmie Rodgers' "Blue Yodel No. 9,"
his voice a skipping stone over the yard birds and crows
accompanying his tune where Louis Armstrong's trumpet

should have been. Last Christmas morning he remembered me,
called me by my name and not my father's, his eyes desperate
to stave off the post-operative delirium after doctors pinned

his fractured hip. Winter has washed out the corduroy
fields, Bahia edging the land, briar and brambles of undergrowth.

I wanted to tell him, *Papaw, these lines become hard rows*

to hoe, that I'd trade all the words I've planted in these poems
for and about people who'll never read them, to work
his land, those acres I will not inherit.

Elegy While Working for Cash Landscaping

There's enough sweat in my clothes to wring out and overflow
a three-gallon bucket. But I love the lines,

the demarcation of what's to come and what will never be again.
The lie of it all. I love watching the old man shirk his work,

him drinking coffee in a rocking chair, a skein of coffee oil
and yard dust in his cup, the widows who keep him filled

to the brim. *Customer Relations, son,* he says when I give him a hard time
driving down White Sulphur Springs Road with its ditches

full of trash like a mote between us and the pumpjacks clacking sputters of oil
on our way to the next yard. He tells me about the riverboat casinos

in Natchez, how the slot machines' handles pull smooth. From the yard,
Granny's kitchen smells like sweet cornbread and pork-chop grease.

Soon he'll be heading out toward the Mississippi River, his pockets full
of widowed women's Social Security. He'll nickel and dime slots

with such care, like a mother spooning mushed peas into an infant's mouth,
as if he cared enough for the machine something might change.

Going Slow

Skunks and hogs rummage the family garden
   in the back forty behind my father's house.
The memories I have of my father's
   father revolve around that dirt:
him riding me up and down turnrows
   in his tractor bucket when I was small,
directing my hands as I tilled a row,
   his hands hard enough to smooth
a hoe handle like sand paper, how
   I never saw him hurried, how
he wobbled slowly behind us in the fields.
   He would have been happy to die
in that garden hunkered over some lima beans
   and purple hull peas, to leave this world
with a bushel in a bucket instead of piss
   in a catheter. I wasn't there when my father
tilled under the last crop he'd ever share
   with his father, wasn't there to see the blade
rip and bury what they hadn't picked. Dad talks
   about shoving down grandpa's old deer blind
under the oak that's between the potatoes
   and squash. We both know he won't do it,
both know too much is lost to a machine.
   My father will leave it to the earth to take
on its own power, in its own time.

Christmas Elegy with a Foot Out the Door

We drive our usual thousand miles, our children
in their wrinkled clothes and food-stained mouths,

Thatcher, older now, sitting in his booster seat with a Walkie
Talkie pressed against his teeth and the other held out

toward my wife and me like a megaphone proclaiming,
I've got to pee. Over. 10-4, good buddy? as he goes on

to pee himself there in the back, and I stop and root
through luggage for clean Superman underwear at a Texaco

and somehow know this trip will be the last time I'll see
my grandfather alive—this man who sees me as his own,

who sharpened my pocket knives, held squirrels for me to gut, catfish
to skin, who rambled backroads with gas cans looking

for me in the ditches. Now he's a felled hickory rotting,
laid over in his rocking chair waiting for my mother

to fix him a plate of dressing and cranberry sauce
and lemon pie, waiting for my grandmother

to brew a pot of coffee, pour it into the mug that has felt his lips
more than she has. He gives my son a guitar

he scavenged from the dump. *We don't have the room*
for it this trip, I tell him as I hang it back

on the wall. He offers me his own guitar, the one my fingers fought
those teenage years I lived with him. *Maybe next trip,* I say.

My daughter doesn't know this is her first Christmas,
probably his last goodbye to her. She hops

on his soft lap while he holds her hands, sings so she'll rock
her head and laugh. He tries to stand to say goodbye

as the labor of long years waters the stone of his hands
to bread that I shake while turning away

toward the truck I'll take across the country,
knowing this last look is the easy memory.

The Faith Healer Comes for a Summer Revival

Praise songs soaked threadbare
carpet and pews with *When I die, hallelujah,*
by and by, I'll fly away, and grandma would clap
her hands on the down beat as hard as her arthritis allowed.

The faith healer would call the lame
and afflicted to meet him there at the altar.

Her hairspray would sit in my nose
as she passed me on her way into the aisle.

One pew after another, she grew straighter.

Eyes closed and wet, through the calamity
she felt her way down the aisle with her hands.

The hands of others pushed her along,
until she swam the river of fingers
to offer the rheumatoid to the healer.

In that great a-gettin up morning, fare thee well

swelled the walls as the evangelist rubbed
the Lord's healing onto her knot-bulged knuckles
and offered up her hands to the air. *Sister,* he'd shout
letting the hands go,
will you claim this victory?
And she did, over and over.

Stretch forth your hands to your beloved sister,
he wailed into the microphone.

What heaviness her lifted arms must have taken
as they slunk down onto her belief.
What mercy when he reached
out and held the weight of it all up at her elbows.

Edified in the collective faith and healing
power of belief,
                                    she held out her hands for days

but by Wednesday,
                                    she would weep in the kitchen
                                    over a sealed Mason jar of mayhaw jelly.

Before the Quadruple Bypass, the Preacher Comes to Pray

As late as Y2K, folks in LaSalle Parish expected preachers to make house calls between Sunday services. Pastor Davis came out to our place four or five times a year then. My grandma would wake me and papaw up from our naps, pot roast, rice and gravy, and cornbread still smelling up the house. We'd all watch the second quarter of the Saints game, then go out to the porch and sip coffee at halftime, the horse nickering for peppermints at the pasture gate, hummingbirds flying back and forth from the porch to the mimosa tree, the dog running off the birds pecking for seeds. Pastor Davis always just sat there, blowing his cup of coffee, staring off into our thicket like he was going to see something. Grandad would tell him about the weather, about the time he drove a hundred head of cattle from his home on Old River all through the town, about how the fishing's no good the days the heifers lay on their legs. When Pastor Davis was ready to leave, he'd ask my grandad if it'd be okay if he said a word of prayer. And granddad would tell him, *Hell, preacher, that'd be all right.* Pastor Davis would drop his hands around the back of my grandad's neck and pray that the good Lord would heal his heart disease, would be with him when the surgeons open his chest, root around in the heart's valves and tendons. The breeze cooled what coffee was left. Granddad's comb-over unknotted. His eyes clenched shut just as tight as a believer's.

Elegy with Tobacco Spit and Little Debbie Cakes

Those mornings were all fog falling down the Aimwell hills, all dog howls
through the hardwood bottoms as they ran bucks, all C.B. talk,

a tennis ball kabobbed onto the six-foot antenna that banged against
the truck's cab, tobacco spit cups by the gear shift, my bolt action

rifle in the gun rack, his shotgun with double-aught buckshot
between us pointing at the floorboard, orange vests

and Little Debbie cakes strewed across the seat, cousin Jerry
and Red Carter radioing *10-4s* and *overs* and *Get your ass over*

to Two-Mile Cutoff, Spanky behind the truck on a three-wheeler,
all of us chasing hounds chasing deer, trying to make it

to the nearest pipeline for a shot, my grandfather's cowboy hat
pushed back behind his ears and him cussing that Dodge

that wouldn't shift into second. Those mornings were all failure,
and I came up believing maybe things aren't supposed to work:

a doe throwing those walker hounds, us losing a dog
and having to wander gravel and logging trams looking

for a lost dog under the moonlight that stumbled
through the loblolly, to carry it out on my shoulders, its breath

alchemizing the peach fuzz down my neck to ice.
I came up believing maybe it was right that we could never steady

a rifle from a drifting truck's rolled down window, November
pouring into the cab, the cold watering my eyes as I squinted

through crosshairs as deer and hounds passed, the mornings
I pulled the trigger, mornings I didn't. Even now I see it all passing,

all that life that wouldn't stop, how I'd cup my hands
over the Dodge's vent to thaw, how I couldn't sleep the night

before thinking about how my grandpa was going to stuff
fast-food napkins into his cowboy hat's headband and drop it

onto my head, the weight of it on my ears. But the hounds'
barks just trailed off into the distance past brown fur snagged

in a patch of briars. Those days passing through us
were just a fading bruise a rifle kicked into my shoulder.

For Edith, From the North Country

. . . keep her from the howlin' winds
—Dylan

You came too fast for medicine, nearly delivered en route
while your mother screamed to drive faster as I bobsledded
our car down the ice of South Hill. Your brother rang the bell
behind the nurses' station that tumbled your name down
every hall. That evening, still glazed with womb, you lay across
your mother's breasts, the two of you asleep in front of the room's
one window. From my phone, Dylan sang for a North Country girl.
The New Year's snow slid sideways over the glass. Wind raged
elms and larch. You wore a sleep-smile. Dylan blew his harmonica.
It doesn't snow in Florida. Someday you'll look back and wonder why
your father lullabied you with lyrics of winter storming and coats
so warm. But know you arrived in a blizzard 3,000 miles away,
that you slept across your mother's chest a few feet from the gusted
flakes, your glazed-purple skin from the last world already fading.

3

I'm going to need a new pair of shoes
when I get through walking these blues

—FATS DOMINO

On Thomas Wolfe's Assertion of Home After Having Lived a Long Time 3,000 Miles Away

I'm thinking of all that country

between me and the Lower Mississippi River Delta:

That town in West Texas

where cattle outnumber people. Its great brown plains of dirt

peppered by twitching black hide and the horseflies

scratching their legs

beside the oil-slick water puddle

under a gas pump at the Sinclair. There's a hotel

in New Mexico where the sun takes up the whole window,

kids tossing rocks across the road

at the traffic sign in front of a truck stop's ghost.

Colorado is different than you think:

you can watch black clouds scratch
the earth's back as they swirl the plains
east of Denver.

There's the Crow Nation's land in Montana

where the chain of Dairy Queens end

just before the Clark Fork River crosses your eyes. Land in Idaho

is on the rise, 18-wheelers hauling craft beer

from Portland share the road

with cattle trailers bursting with haybales.

My eyes are full satchels of snake oil.

The pictures of these miles held
against the back
of my eyelids I'd give away
to make room for the older images.
I blink
and blink
cycling through them

looking for that one in LaSalle Parish
where I'm washing

fresh tar off my father's Chevy step-side fender wells,

my little sister in the truck bed,

a purple bath towel tied
around her head and her saying,

Do you like my new hair, Bubba? steel toes shining through

the busted leather of my father's work boots as he lies

under my mother's car

changing the Bonneville's oil, my mother

in front of the trailer troweling holes for petunias

and elephant ears

how the sweet gum held

the sun all day in its

branches.

I keep blinking keep looking for it there behind the lids of my eyes.

I want to answer my sister, to tell her,

Yes,

oh yes,

to find a branch to comb that hair

before she unties it for good.

Keats in LaSalle Parish

—after Philip Levine

The black eyes of the plum tree plunge to the ground. They squish
between my children's toes. This late wind pulls scabs

from the crape myrtle that lodge in the mimosa limbs
hanging over the dry-rot of an old water hose.

This is now just my grandmother's land, just her trailer house.
She swishes a jar of sugar water and red food dye

to pour into the hummingbird feeder. These few trees that remain
give only a little midday shade as she hands me a cup of coffee,

sits on the swing to talk about the ones we've lost: the red oak
the lightning took, the hickory some hurricane felled,

the rest of the front lot mostly a pasture now after James Larry sold
the timber to International Paper. The dogwood she misses most.

It would've been in bloom about now, she says, mistaken, sipping her cup. I tell her
it's a hard place. *The only land in this country not on the rise*,

she laughs. I want to tell her about Keats, about the veil
of soul making, but she can't stop herself

from reminding me about the Lord, about that light burden,
that easy yoke. Across the road, Jack Ziggler starts his evening

target practice sighting in another rifle. James Larry has sold off more
of his timber, this time from the plot behind her trailer.

A white updraft skulks across LaSalle over to Catahoula Parish.
She blows her coffee. The slack of orange flagging

the loggers tied around the trees whip in the breeze against tree bark
like a father's belt across his son's hide.

Elegy Unfolding as I Leave Spokane, WA

To head back south through the switchbacked
        Lolo National Forest, there'll be the Clark Fork
    you read about in Hugo's poems, a sign off I-90
        for Philipsburg, the big sky country of Montana
and Wyoming and through Denver construction,
        onto the pass dividing the last bit
    of mountains in New Mexico, until I finally come
        to the first heat lightning storming
the east Texas sky like those that wallowed across
        Baton Rouge up to St. Francisville.

I'll remember little of the West, but I'll see
        the one evening after driving home
    from Cheney to Spokane, when I turned on
        the record player and my son, Thatch,
and I danced to Buckwheat Zydeco, how he tried
        to keep up with the lyrics to "Tutti Fruiti,"
    hot grease in the Dutch oven, chicken brining
        in buttermilk, a bowl of flour seasoned
with paprika, Slap Ya Mama, white pepper and cayenne.

I'll think of Wayne Toups singing about walking down
        sugar cane roads as I dropped the thighs
    into the grease, how I cut the potatoes singing,
        I'm going up the country by cold sleet and snow,
no telling how much further I may go, as Nic and Thatch shuffled
        out of time to Mississippi John Hurt's thumb
    walking the bass line. I'll remember
        Nic smiling at Thatch. All those miles
will spring back like a let go rubber band,
        and everything I love will catch in that melody,
    in the two of them dancing over a mess of toys in the floor.

Coming Home: Most Things Change Except Humidity

This feeling must've come after a rain. Steam sauntered
off potholes in the driveway from water nearly boiling,
trash and limbs clogged drainage ditches, birds in the yard

pecked for worms the afternoon shower washed up.
The whole yard felt like walking out of a shower
with the bathroom door closed. Beads of sweat

dropped down the bark of red maple, hackberry
and magnolias. A film of pollen crusted over the top
of backwater, oil sheening the road. It was the first day

back home in years. Everything the steam smothered
had changed, but my lungs had the familiar full feel
of humidity again. I felt too large for this body as I breathed

heavy air at sea level, felt nearly too large for the roads
wandering across the swamps, canopied by another afternoon
lightning storm, my mother in the yard walking toward me,

my grandmother in the doorway yelling, *Where y'at, boy?*
Come here so I can see you. All of us holding each other
in our arms, our fogged eyeglasses in our hands.

Front Porch at 775 Hanger Road

Squirrel barks rattling
your eardrum, red prism

of sugar water for the hummingbirds,
the Doberman your dad brought home

from the dump, ears mangled
from a botched clipping,

you don't know what makes a place,
so much of it gone or leaving.

Boards sealed with 10W-30 bend under you.
Every nail comes to nothing in the rot.

Your hammer's kisses yellowing with pollen,
turning their eyes back to this world.

The swing still swings.
The pitted chain thinned.

You move a new link
into the hook and sit

for a time trying to remain.
The chain scraping

against crickets and frogs
that stretch their voices into dusk.

Elegy with Steel Wool Plugging Holes

Every bit of ten years ago, I spent a day
    with an extension ladder propped up the side

of my grandparents' single-wide with a long-pole
    paint roller rolling GacoRoof onto their trailer

to keep the electric bill down. Not long after,
    I spent another day, not long before I left for good,

on my hands and knees with steel wool and duct tape
    plugging holes in the closets and pantry to keep the rats

out. My mother called me last December
    before I boarded a plane home from Spokane

to New Orleans to say Papaw fell and broke
    his hip helping Granny tote groceries inside,

that the day before, the old man had been up
    on a ladder trying to put a new coat on the roof

after the Louisiana summers nearly rotted mine
    off. I lived with Granny and Papaw the six teenage years

I spent refusing to split time between my parents'
    new homes. Those days, rats stirred mostly at night,

the living room walls riled and alive with their thumps,
    how they clawed themselves into our lives. On the phone,

Mom said Granny had to leave Papaw at the hospital
to start driving home before it got too dark for her to see

the road. And I called Granny after landing to check in. I listened
for a while to her voice trailing off into the grog

of the last days. Then I found myself listening past it,
listening for the scratching noise of the rats I knew

might be behind her on the couch. I wondered about the steel wool
plugging holes, wondered how long it would hold.

Elegy with Dementia and the Diaspora of Family

This is not your home, so why not pass by?
  Your parents' trailer sold and hauled off.
Look at the azalea bush where your room
  was once, the birdbath where your sister
used to sleep. All that's left is the cement
  you and your father poured for the floor
of his workshop. It's all gone: the table
  and jig and miter saws, the extension
cords, and air compressors. It's only gray
  cement and knotty boards soft with rot
after your uncle used it for a meth shed.
  Do not stop at the pond to wet a line.
The large-mouthed hook-scarred bass
  you caught and released are gone. Do not look
for your tree house or remember lifting
  its boards to your father, the nails pinched
between thumb and finger, the flesh a sheet
  of tin opened. It's all pasture now speckled
with cow patties. Do not go inside your grand-
  parents' trailer, your teenage room down the hall.
Drive, instead, to the nursing home, as much
  your family's as anything now. See him there.
Good days, he remembers the two of you
  making hay while the sun shone. Other days,
all the years he built will pass by. Stop there.
  Offer him your hand. Tell him who you are.
Tell him again if you must. Tell him
  again and again and do not stop.

Spending the Summer Back in Louisiana with All My Stuff Still in Washington

Heat waves vibrate out the throats of sugar cane.
From Baton Rouge to New Orleans,
Clifton Chenier sings about coming home
to his mother. His voice an accordion
prowl from the speakers and out
the open truck windows.

July melts tar from the road, boils what's left
of yesterday's storm brimming in potholes.

Louisiana was never meant to be driven.
Four of the five longest bridges in America
sweat above the state's lakes and swamps.

We drive the Twin Span Bridge over
the Pontchartrain from New Orleans back to Addis.

Silver water washes the eggshell sky.
The old bridge beside us is a ruined fossil
that kneels on knees that Katrina buckled years ago.

In the evening, Tab and Willie sing "Rainy Day Blues"
as another shower wets the cane. Fires somersault
Douglas fir in Washington while waterlogged moss
leans these limbs in closer, and I can touch so little that I own,
that I need hardly anything other than all this water.

Spokane, WA

—for Kurt Olsen

Soon we'll leave that poetry class we're walking toward
and go our own way, but I'm at Boots
in Spokane now with Kurt. We started with coffee,
but are now on to cheap beer, scratching out words
in poems, drawing exclamation points,
growling about work and time. He's down again.
I'm down again. The beer wallows in our guts,
fumbles across our cords of blood.
I grab from him his bummed Golbarth collection
we were assigned to read but were too poor to buy.
We gripe about Goldbarth, how much work
he asks of us so late in the day, so late in the year,
so late into our bar tab. I do not know that this
is the last time I'll see Kurt. I'm happy
to pack tobacco into my pipe while he rolls a cigarette.
I complain to him outside that no one told me
how soon it gets dark in the winter in the north.
I am cold. He brags about his Nordic blood.
I don't know this is it. We walk to class. I try to recite Levine.
He tries to recite Lux. He pulls bottom-shelf bourbon
from his backpack, and we pour it into coffee cups.
Bourbon warms my throat, reddens our eyes. I don't tell him
anything important. We try again to remember words
to poems we hold in our throats as long as a memory can last.
He doesn't tell me anything important. The street lights
try to decide whether to burn or sleep. Their click and hum,
click and hum is a decision drawn out as our feet crunch
across that new ice the city will bruise with traffic oil
and tobacco spit. Our words are a sour mist lingering a moment
on a crosswalk, then crossing on, our last few steps widening still.

In the Pasture Between What Was Your Grandparents' House and Aunt's House After They Have All Moved On

There's that 1980s satellite dish the size
        of a futon sitting in the field and pointing
    to what, surely, was once a signal behind
the bluebird jacket of sky. Twenty yards away,
        those concrete steps lead to a front door of a trailer
    that's gone. Scale them now. Stand on that top step to nowhere.
        A horse will nicker for peppermints and apples,
    will rub his blazed snout against your two hands
        that will grope for something to hold.

Job 13:21

Some say a man needs dirt and oil under his fingernails, say the nails
need be gnawed down to the bed, say the hands need blisters

from swinging a hammer and cranking twine twirled around outboard
motors, say they aren't meant to idle, say they aren't meant to spare

the rod, say they should come down against a child's cheek, the back
of the head, say the hands should grip with care the leather belt

or tree switch and swing them in disciple, say the clap of the belt
should be as loud as the clap of worship on Sunday mornings,

say hands are meant to be raised in surrender as all the sinners cry out,
Here I am, Lord. You can use me, all the children hiding under pews

with Hot-Wheels, their skin belt-toughened, are too afraid to look at the hands
lifted in praise for fear that it might all come back down upon them.

Elegy with a Brush Hook and Machete

—for Steve

Remember when we almost drowned in '03,
        the woods so thick, we only knew the rainstorm

by sound of thunder and violence of the creek,
        how every day I'd take you to the Stop-N-Go

for your case of Natty Lights? Think back to summertime,
        when after lunch, you'd pull your shirt off and wring it

in your hands and count off *one beer*, wring some more,
        two beers, how in July you'd sweat all the way through

last night's binge. Think back to when we chopped paths
        across hardwood bottoms for skidders to plow

makeshift roads for Justiss Oil's pumpjacks to suck
        black snot the earth doesn't blow. I wanted to call

in sick every day, to feel the sunrise through
        my bedroom pane instead of the company

truck's windshield. But this isn't about that.
        What was I? Eighteen? Drinking creamy coffee

the color of soupy dishwater the callouses
        of my hands sanding the white Styrofoam cup,

whiskey from a flask stirred into yours. I grew
        to welcome the start of a day filing blades,

the rhythm I'd find scraping down, down, up and over.
    I didn't care like you did for squaring drill sites

with double-knots of orange flagging for the loggers,
    how we kneeled, panting in the dirt, how you would pan

your head to take inventory of the beech and white oaks
    rooted inside the flagged-off square. I can't forget

you walking down the orange line touching all
    those trees we sentenced to the chainsaws, and didn't see

that each day was another flag tied around you.
    But what did it matter, Steve, which tree we marked

for loggers to fell, which sapling we ourselves chopped
    with machetes. Did the thicket not return what we gave?

Did the thorn limbs and briars not cut your flesh
    into estuaries of brackish pink creeks

of sweat and blood? Nothing changes much, does it,
    Steve? I'm filing an edge on a brush hook

for the first time in years and still hear you yelling
    at me, *Not like that, Smith. Just give the damn thing to me.*

We spent our days counting off paces, eyeballing
    a hundred yards within a few feet, but I don't think

I have the same distance in me. If I count off
        these paces, where does a record go? Those days,

I dreamt that John the Revelator mistook us
        for Death, the old Chevy a pale horse, us wheeling

those blades through chokecherry and wild honey locust,
        water vines crawling behind us. But I don't know

of any Hell that followed that wasn't there before.
        I never learned much as a surveyor that I didn't

already know: how calloused hands have a way
        of smoothing wood, or else how there's markers

all over this country, how sometimes a fence
        is all we have to pass down.

Just Music

We sang the songs of childhood
Hymns of faith that made us strong

—"Will the Circle Be Unbroken"

There was music there: Indian head woodpeckers
drilling hickory bark, crows and chicken hawks

cawing above the field in front of the parish dumps
where International Paper clear-cut slash pine—music

from D in the shed in the yard strumming Brown Eyed Girl"
with a Mexican Stratocaster, him groping its neck

for the next right chord and on to "Born on the Bayou"—
music in the timing of our feet snapping limbs and leaves

on our way through the river birch and cottonwood
to the dry creek bed, in the whacks of our machetes

into water vines hanging from red oak—music in yardwork,
my aunt whistling "Give Me That Old-Time Religion"

while she gathered leaves to burn, the whoosh of my hands
scarring 16th notes into red cedar with sandpaper,

my father thudding his nail gun on the downbeats
like a kick drum, one grandfather on his hands

and knees picking lima beans singing "There Will Be
Peace in the Valley" another grandfather hunkered down

over summer squash singing “Tonight the Bottle Let Me Down”—
music in the clacking top of the coffee maker dancing

above the steam’s pressure, in the timbre of a voice
when it called out to a visitor, *Get you a cup; sit a spell*—

in the trembling from a Hammond B-3 when we lost
another of the old folk—the congregation singing

about a circle unbroken in the sky, Lord, in the sky
that I don’t know much beyond. There’s something

unbroken in my mouth, in the way I ask Mama
if she wants another cup of coffee, how I sing

the hymns from the clapboard churches and fields
without having to believe in anything beyond this throat,

this air that stops for a moment in these lungs then moves out
away from me on and on in the sky, Lord, in the sky.

Wreckage

I am merely a man dressing in the dark
because that is what a man is

—Phil Levine

The day Nichole birthed Thatcher, my father slipped
me a hundred-dollar bill, pulled me to the side
of the hospital room, full to the gills with family,
and passed it to me like the charity embarrassed him.

I know you've had to take a few days off work for this,
he told me, our hands both fumbling
in our pants' pockets. I can only think of three
other times he freely spent so much on me:

an 870 Express Remington .12 gauge and Savage
bolt-action .270, both Christmas presents
when I was too young to shoulder them,
and a used S-10 Chevy for graduation.

The money he used for the S-10 was mine,
    though. Money I made handing tools up

extension ladders to him, holding the butts
    of tape measures, spackling the cracks of wood
paneling we would soon paint. The better part

    of the year we spent on that house and an acre
where we cleared a thicket of briars and pines, pushed
    around stumps and red clay with a Cat dozer

until we lost the light and fumbled through
    the grassless yard, our boots caked with mud
like biscuit dough on Saturday morning hands,

    and crossed the road to his parents' house where
my sister and I stayed on our days with him after
    my mother served those divorce papers.

We hardly lived there before he remarried
    and moved across town. He said he'd put
my share of the money from the flipped house away.

I don't hunt anymore, not since the preacher
        in West Ouachita Parish stole and pawned
    my guns. I don't miss the recoil against my shoulder,
the ring in my ears that lasted for days, the unforgivable
        act of winging a duck or shooting a deer in the gut,
    to track a wounded animal till I lost the day, to lie
in bed hoping the coyotes would have better luck, that something
        could come from taking a life. But I do miss the sun rising over
    Catahoula lake, the flutter of mallard and gadwall wings over
the duckblind before first-light, the honks of geese crossing
        under moonbeams, the tightness of Neoprene chest waders
    and gloves, how all the fathers and sons of LaSalle Parish
in the moment the sun bludgeoned the lake horizon forgot
        to shoot their guns and just watched the waves crest orange
    in the new day's light, the turkey vultures still asleep
in cypress limbs, decoys anchored in front of blinds,
        covered in frost throwing prisms of light over everything.

I worked through high school bussing tables and frying oysters,
  clams, catfish, and shrimp at Buddy's Fish Fin, lowered

the S-10's suspension three inches, bought low-profile tires,
  chrome wheels, kept stacks of *J.C. Whitney* and *Popular*

Mechanic's catalogues by my bed. My father never kept a vehicle
  long. When he saw the next best thing, he'd just trade up

what he had. I cashed my checks every Thursday at Big Star Grocery,
  pieced that pickup together one payday at a time.

They drain Catahoula Lake every spring to let the vegetation grow
for the ducks in the winter. Swarms of men teaming like termites
wallow around in the black mud building or repairing duckblinds. I couldn't
afford a boat, so my blind was wading distance from the landing where

my S-10, squatted above its wheels, sat bellow all the jacked-up
4-wheel drives. Thomas, Chase, and I were fed up with hauling
cypress boards and treated posts from the landing to where we built
the blind. I eased that S-10 off into black water ankle-deep, made it fifty feet

and bogged down past the doors, crawled out the window, dug down
to the ball hitch. Chase got his Tacoma to pull me out and sunk
that truck, too. We sat there into the night, swatting mosquitoes,
waiting for the flashing lights of a wrecker to yank us out.

The S-10 finally had enough
                                        on Valentine's Day 2008.
          I left it on the shoulder
of I-20 between Shreveport
                                        and Monroe. A few days later,
I rounded up   a flat-bed
            trailer   and Scott,
                                                      Mayo,
              and I shoved it up the ramps,
hauled it
              to a mechanic
          who scrapped it for parts.

I meant to put the hundred dollars my father slipped me
in the hospital room away, to start a college fund
for Thatcher. All these years later, I don't remember now
where the money went: a student loan bill, water bill,
rent, milk and eggs. But my wife and I put money away dollars
at a time for our children to go to college. We tell them to pick
out toys in the store for when we have the cash. And they're happy
to do so, to hold a plastic truck, to push it, still in its box down
the store aisle, to say, *See, dad. It works like this! This is what it'll do*
when we can get it. So much comes to nothing, ends with a wrecker
or just fizzles out. But I tell them, *Next time*. And sometimes I'm right.

Thatcher Starts First Grade

Already, in his mind, he is passing away
from this house, from this once kindergarten body

scabbed with blood
hardening.
He is imagining himself

as this new thing.

This first-grade body that he has earned

through the growing pains

that just this week drove him
to our bed: his mother's voice
in his ear. My hand on his thigh that's aflame

with a bind of ligaments wrestling their elasticity,
and the next day he would ask us to measure him again,

I must have grown
enough now to not be so small.

This morning of a new school year, he constructs his hair,
admires it for a moment until the creek
of his lips overrun their banks into a frown.

Dad, I can't wear my hair this crazy
on my first day.

He hands me the pomade to fix it. And I do, looking down
to find which way the crown of his hair spirals out,

making the part, pushing a comb-over of blond
across his head away from me.
Not that normal, Dad.
It needs to still be a little crazy.

It is time to go. He runs around the house

pulling down light switches. He lopes
past me, stopping
only long enough for a picture I'll later share with his mother.

Then he holds out his hand for mine: his grip cinched
around three of my fingers.

Last year, his mother was a part of his first leaving.

She held his hand as I followed behind them,
melancholic
in the already swirling heat,

her showing to him the way, him only a half-step behind

and with only a faint drag between her arm and his.

The neighborhood children are wiping sleep from their eyes.

I asked him if he was ready for all of this:
a new school,
a new grade.

Children, holding their new supplies, waddle toward the bus.

He sucks a deep breath of fog into his chest.

The bus's stop sign flared out

and flashing as he starts to step, then turns

to give me a last hug, then spins again away

from me, my arms that were just around his body
are now to him only phantom pains from some other time.

For Edith in Her Crib

Little bird, little starling scraping your wings
 against the oak slats of your crib in the flood

light, tears falling back into your body
 through its open beak, I would pull a sunrise

from my chest to wash away this dream waking
 you. I have carried you so far. You've seen twelve states,

crossed five thousand miles before you knew the word
 for the pain in your stomach or the fire of larch

waterfalling down the Cascades or the taste of saltwater
 in your mouth on Florida's Forgotten Coast.

Even now, in the long moments it takes you
 to stumble your foot in front of the other

like a three-a.m. field sobriety test, this life you know
 with me speeds away to some end that we

can't see. These moments between your brother's bed
 and your crib, the shadows of the crape myrtle branches

across your face and mine as you lay your head
 at the bottom of my throat and sigh and thread

your fingers through my beard until they fall back down
 in sleep—these moments are my breath you try to catch

in your hand when I'm carrying you out into the cold,
 the molts of our lives tangling for just a moment.

Reprise

Elegy for Delta Summers

There's a moment in a field when dusk squats low
over the hickory and loblolly, over turnrows

and rusted tillers and tractors and hoes, when the cicadas
lurch their lives out into air, crickets smashing their mouths

against the steaming remains of the day, when it all cascades
into silence like a bad station fading out the truck window

as your mother's inside stirring a roux, your sister on her tiptoes
setting the table, your father shucking off the day's labor,

leaving it in the mud and sweat and sawdust-caked clothes
on the bathroom floor, when the breeze settles, the dust falls

back into rows and awaiting the dew, when you don't know
if your eyes are open or closed, a moment your grandfather

will crumble leftover cornbread into a bowl of milk as the white
water of your grandmother's car beams climb over your head

while she pulls back down the drive from a prayer meeting,
a moment when nothing is really lit or unseen. Hold out

your hands to this. A patch of garden, the hog fattened for winter
asleep in its water trough, to the walker hounds in their pens

wetting their noses with their tongues. Hold your hands out
to this day a little longer. You'll come back here years from now

to stand in what was a worn turnrow, but they'll be no tractor
    or hog, no squash or tomatoes, they'll be no supper on the table.

Even the cicadas are gone. It'll be years before another brood
    will emerge. And besides you, they're all that's coming back.

ACKNOWLEDGMENTS

I'm grateful to the editors of the following magazines who first published these poems.

"Elegy for a Brush Hook and Machete" *Poetry* (June 2019)
"Christmas Elegy with a Foot Out the Door" *Willow Springs* 83 (Winter 2019)
"Elegy in Times of Dementia and Family Diaspora" *Prairie Schooner* 92 no. 3 (Fall 2018)
"Elegy with Steel Wool Plugging Rat Holes" *Prairie Schooner* 92 no. 3 (Fall 2018)
"Elegy Uprooted from the Wet Soil" *Louisiana Literature* 35, no. 2 (Fall–Winter 2018)
"Elegy for the Pond" *Sugar House Review* (Winter 2018)
"Front Porch at 775 Hanger Road" *Louisiana Literature* 34, no. 1 (Spring–Summer 2017)
"Gulf State Elegy Unfolding Under Evacuation" *Mississippi Review* (Summer 2018)
"Heat Lightning" *Louisiana Literature* 35, no. 2 (Fall–Winter 2018)
"Hurricane Parties" *The McNeese Review* (Spring 2017)
"Louisiana Wetland Elegy Taken Out to Sea" *The Raleigh Review* 7, no. 2 (Fall 2017)
"Ode for Delta Summers" *South 85* (Spring–Summer 2016)
"Picking Up Cans" *San Pedro River Review* (Spring 2018)
"The Faith Healer Comes for a Summer Revival" *The McNeese Review* (Spring 2017)
"Up and Over the Mountain" *Permafrost* 38, no. 1 (Winter 2016)

"Just Music," "Elegy for Delta Summers," and "Up and Over the Mountain" are forthcoming in the anthology *Burden/Boon: Writings on Heritage*.

ACKNOWLEDGMENTS

"Flash Flood, Mid-August," "Hurricane Parties," and "Louisiana Wetland Elegy" are forthcoming in *Southern Ecology Anthology*.

"Elegy for Delta Summers," "Flash Flood, Mid-August," "Flash Flood, Mid-August Baton Rouge," "Hurricane Parties," "Picking Up Cans," "Up and Over the Mountain," "Elegy for the Family Tractor," "Going Slow," "Wreckage," and "Ode for Delta Summers" appeared in the chapbook *Delta Summers* published by Yellow Flag Press (2016).